THE Dissolving ISLAND

Also by David Rigsbee

Invited Guest: An Anthology of Twentieth Century Southern
        Poetry (Ed. with Steven Ford Brown)
Greatest Hits: 1975-2000
Scenes on an Obelisk
Styles of Ruin: Joseph Brodsky and the Postmodernist Elegy
A Skeptic's Notebook: Longer Poems
Trailers (with Carol Burch-Brown)
Your Heart Will Fly Away
An Answering Music: On the Poetry of Carolyn Kizer (Ed.)
The Hopper Light
The Ardis Anthology of New American Poetry (Ed. with
        Ellendea Proffer)
Stamping Ground

THE  ISLAND

– P O E M S –

DAVID RIGSBEE

BkMk Press
University of Missouri-Kansas City

BkMk Press
University of Missouri-Kansas City
5100 Rockhill Road
Kansas City, Missouri 64110
(816) 235-2558 (voice)
(816) 235-2611 (fax)
www.umkc.edu/bkmk/
bkmk@umkc.edu

MAC
MISSOURI ARTS COUNCIL

Financial assistance for this book has been provided by the
Missouri Arts Council, a state agency.

Cover painting: "The Dissolving Island" by Jill Bullitt (1998)
Cover design: Margaret Rabb
Additional design: Susan L. Schurman
Production staff: Ben Furnish (managing editor); Susan L.
Schurman (assistant managing editor); Bill Beeson, Dennis
Conrow, Matt Ehrhorn, Lisieux Huelman, Jessica Hylan, Emily
Iorg.
Printing by Josten's, Topeka, Kansas

Library of Congress Cataloging-in-Publication Data

Rigsbee, David.
        The dissolving island / David Rigsbee.
              p. cm.
ISBN 1-886157-43-X

PS3568.I375D57 2003   2003014713
811'.54--dc22

*For Makaiya and Jill
and in memory of Dougald McMillan (1938-1999)*

Acknowledgments

I wish to thank the editors of the following publications in which many of these poems first appeared: *The American Poetry Review, Birdsuit* (U.K.), *The Brooklyn Rail, Cimarron Review, The Cortland Review, Exquisite Corpse, The Fiddlehead* (Canada), *The Greensboro Review, The Journal, The Literary Review, The Marlboro Review, The New Orleans Review, The North Atlantic Review, The Ohio Review, Sewanee Review, Simple Vows, Solo, The South Carolina Review, The Southern Humanities Review, The Southern Review, The Texas Review, The William and Mary Review, Willow Springs.*

Pudding House Publications for a chapbook, *Scenes on an Obelisk*, in which "Realm of Day" first appeared.

I would also like to express my gratitude to the Virginia Commission on the Arts, to the National Endowment for the Humanities and the American Academy in Rome for fellowship assistance, to the Djerassi Foundation and the Weymouth Center for the Arts for residencies, to the Academy of American Poets for a prize, and to *Willow Springs* for the Vachel Lindsay Award.

Contents

The Garden of Catherine Blake
for Jill

Cloud and earth converge like banners of geese,
both undulant, assimilable
each to the other.
Though I draw the horizon line
with the eye's rule, without
question, they pass into each other.

Easter again, and this sod
with its sticks and rubbish,
its whirled grasses, as if a mower demon
had whetted his scythe to reveal our grave,
is even more of paradise than when
God rose
from the cave of the brain
and leapt to tongue like a petrel
astounding the grave academics!

I do not doubt the light behind the trees
secures a meaning and fastens it
to our despair. Or that the same slant light
skimming across the boards
where we talked the winter warm,
fanned by the wings of seraphs,
is all the unendurable fullness
of this sweet paradise.

From which, so suddenly, we rise
and join the air, exalting the matter
spread below in its circular struggle,
that was our home awhile.

Only Heaven

A rabbit turns the aerial of his ears.
He? The grass lays back, plowed
with the approach of . . .
One doesn't know what the approach is of.
His empty wit.

It is a postmodern evening in America.
It is after a lot of things. Now,
the woman cracks the door to make sure
it's him. Only the flesh of summer leaves
blocks the mystery of starlight.

Only a bicycle goes by as he slips
into the lighted crack.
The sound of the chain is seemingly amplified
as it goes from the teeth of the flywheel
to the little teeth
and out again until the sound is lost.

Until the sound is found
again, heightened, the way lovers in an opera
pass the climactic moment to strings
and lapse replaced, knowing the meaning
will be handled properly, as the last
wisps of sound disperse
into the space they used to think

the only heaven.

The Metaphysical Painters

What if, after the tulips' slow ecstasy,
the void? I see
through Magellanic Clouds of veronica,
the amnesiac blankets of dandelions,
how the dark possibility
takes the lawn.

Only yesterday, last week—can't
put my finger on it—there was
a house, its eyes our eyes,
and we were in our houses traveling.
To shovel the past forward
gets us to snow's empery,
and the green swells, in turn,
to meet it.

Therefore, I
can't tell you of the provenance
of summer. The waves slaughter
themselves in rows, the ditch struggles.
They go down because it's nothing,
not the way I would take your shaping hand,
never to take up again
the mating of beauty to cruelty.

Turner's Mists

No sound here. Crickets stand in the grass,
all-sensing, waiting

for the edges of trees to work through,
photons to assemble.

Many were notorious fakes. The Louvre
hung them anyway,

hoping for the mother lode after death—
which never came.

The sky begins, on one side, to assert itself.
Its brand of blue, which in our century

stands for the indifferent, dispenses
meaning, revealing a bay

and implicit in it, ships and commerce.
Such sky, then, looks forward;

even its mist equals only momentary chaos,
out of which land is coming to life,

even though here it edges an ochre smudge
to bridge the frame.

Nevertheless, mist
predominates.

(And what would be the *point* of faking
such meticulous gradations?)

You think, "I know how this will turn out,"
though without assurances,

for when did certainty ever stand or fall
on the burning off of mist,

when whole fleets bound for you stir
under the hope of earth?

My Raven

They say there are always two:
the unnoticed one stands
lookout over the dark highway,
while the other tears
and works gobbets
off the bone
with the pliers of its beak.

You have to look
and look hard, before the other
is revealed, and yet there
it is: fat as a smudge pot,
fanned in and out of sight
by breezes that connect
with the careless leaves.

But the raven in my yard
has no other. Austere
as a Brancusi, it perches
day after day in the elm,
apple, oak, all the trees
that fructify the sightlines
of the yard, occasionally

cawing through, like conscience,
when I have turned from
the unused window to more
transparent things. Perhaps it
means to take care of my
vigilance for me, with its grip

and undeceiving eye.

But shadowing desire, it
will not leave the yard
until I have remade my hunger
and dropped down by the ditch,
in spite of cars and the terror of space,
emerging with enraptured eye,
like one who would eat his fill.

Almost You

I look through the glass and think:
how many lives does this make?
There are the deck chairs, and, yes,
that's a palm—I knew them once—
and the pool that doubles and bathes,
bathes and doubles. Until I too
am double and more, memory
a prism lighting some square—
a small pane of light, surely, but a light.

I'm getting tough and humble.
Isn't this what years are for?
Perhaps I've got it all wrong,
but I don't think so. Uncannily,
I see you now, your shattered flesh
grown transparent, and I wonder,
why have you come when I
have only this barrier to offer,
this glass and this square?

Maybe the past will speak to us,
but we won't speak to the past
any more than a fly on a window
would be, to the window, any more
than a speck. Tough and humble
is what happens: more barriers,
more scraping away, more self-
effacing until the glass is clean.
And no one looks through.

Grayscale

This is the afterlife, that I can say this
while ivy climbs down out of its pot,
and paperwhites, stem-tipped
with pot-scrubber-sponge blossoms
shoot out a stiff, astringent smell
as attention-getting as a hiss. No
explanation lurks behind the odor
to contain its strangeness; no expression
of mine can do more than tell you

of its failures. But how happy the cat
seems, yawning through the plants
transplanted to the apartment world.
Their gray shadows rise and move,
seem sometimes 3-D. Above them,
there's the unmoving shadow of a fence
in a painting, the fence going
to the vanishing point, an empty house,
sentimental, situated on a hill.

There's a scene at every window, too,
and you're not in them, but rather
generalized by this shadow that comes,
courtesy of traffic, and like traffic
leaves, only managing to distinguish
itself momentarily from the ceiling's
unceremonial blank: the insubstantial
anytime, becoming the air of paperwhites,
painted clouds over a painted fence.

But never superior to actual ones
before which winter trees become
skeletal, clapboard houses a few degrees
whiter than anyone had reckoned—
their windows and roofs, by contrast, life-
containing rectangles and parallelograms,
their chimneys channels of access
to an ineffable sky, where you might have
crossed momentarily, the color of smoke.

The Dissolving Island

No signs or announcements
preceded the melting of the beaches.
You went by way of touch. You
were given to think how gravity
misshaped the bodies you encountered.

Clouds skimmed the optic nerve.
The lean shadows of water-striders
marbled the submerged, sunlit
columns whose ruin rose
to the querying snouts of fish.

A litter of shells. Your feet
fit perfectly among them,
much better than any shoe,
and everywhere the bivalve suck,
sand's volcanic bubbles.

You were returning, or, it
seemed a return, for hardly had
the descriptions arrived when
frogs hopped into the darkness
croaking of the profit

that comes of adventure.
Their choir turned gross, inarticulate.
The wet precincts gobbled up
their expressions, as if greetings
converged with farewells.

When the announcement came
to evacuate, the thought grazed you that
        your feeling about starlight had been,
after all, fantasy, not fit to be thought
        the thing it really was, the everyday-less-

        brilliant fires, scrolling backwards,
discounting the dark, dissolving shores,
        declining to chart how it came to be
that the figure and ground changed places,
        that the island slid back to the sea.

White Rainbow

When the fog came through
I didn't doubt for a minute that
I was onto something, and I was
in a hurry to get up the parched hill
where the world finally opened like a cracked fruit.
The sun was just clearing another hill to my right,
its disk rising through the chests of cows
who stood with straw trailing from their mouths.
Already the odor of their flanks
proved too much for a cloud of flies
who, enchanted with the stench, buzzed
like mid-afternoon and made a quivering satellite shade
on the grass, as if to make up for the cows'
oil-drum shadows, beginning now to decline.
I walked quickly and, in an instant, took all this in,
beginning to breathe heavily now
as the grade steepened. Nevertheless I kept to the pace.
Why sink now that the earth's tilt made
shambling a burden? I left that for the body's
self-estranging mechanism to figure and walked on.
To my left there appeared the rare, white rainbow
plunging through fog and trees: a wicket
opening on the sea (sea that was no business
of mine). I looked once, hard, without breaking stride
as the eye of the fog enveloped its own iris,
my look returning sinew and disbelief
against the fog's cataract. But I was late,
could already feel the tedium of repetition in my legs.
Could imagine, in fact, exhausted bodies
merging, out of the fog, with mine:
but why? They crossed the mind's screen,

borne on its fog like something on a thermal.
At the top of one small hill I plunged down
without grace except for an obedience
to surfaces and the apprehension of time compressed
the way a skittish deer starts at a crackle.
The fog came in droplets, washed-out tapestries
that made the road seem like a diorama,
the *trompe l'oeil* hills and cardboard sea.
A hawk floated over, wings stiff as a kite's crosspiece.
One could hear
the cow's echoing voices up and down the hills.
Ridiculous, I thought: the echo of a cow,
but I hadn't time for ridicule. I was walking
like the smudge on a time-exposure
of some vanished landscape whose power once came
from blurred figures—Van Gogh's
potato-gougers, for instance, bent peasants
whose painfully arched flesh
so bluntly plugged them—head first—back
into earth, as to trap them in redundancy,
burrowing, hoeing, scratching their way along,
having not seen clouds in years,
nor troubled with other
than primal assertions. Nor therefore un-bent
and walked about like Athenians
discussing the portent of rainbows, the illusion
of time, the differences between the greater
and the lesser fogs.

Fault Line

Some cows on the path and everywhere scrub
diving into ravines. Somewhere at the labyrinth's end
the sea begins, whose top of fog slides in
every day, then pulls back, like the lid
of a photocopier. At one ravine: the fault line,
snake of rock, a slither across the valley floor.
The path ends here too. Rather discontinues.
Ionic redwood columns, defiantly perpendicular
begin triangulating the hills' downward slopes.

The effect is of a funnel, or a wedge
of speculation, sight caught on the event horizon
and sucked down under
to the thickly dark, tellurian strain of plate-
grinding, chthonic melodramas about to open.
Above, moss and squlchy ground, streamlined
by the absence of wind, an absence like a young cat
dry-throated in an empty house, who continues
to make the plaintive O with its fur face.

Redwoods and their toughened poles
measuring light in cylinders, in gone-over boxcars,
then air rising to the first bands of nothingness,
ring over ring, of thought perhaps—
its equivocal shadow—like shade.
The cows stand on paths that seem
grooves down the side of a hopper,
their hooves staked to the incline
like matchsticks. Doing what cows do.

Which is to give the hikers who happen

upon the thick mailboxes of their heads,
horns extruded, and massive sideways flanks,
a start. You wonder why they lumber the paths at all,
why they return *that* glare. The fault line
hides the fault like weather stripping.
Hikers get past the cows, forget them,
if only to have carried some wholeness
of their own to the bottom, then circled

upward, by paths divided everywhere.

Sketches of Spain

Times were better once,
before I read Spinoza
and felt his logic shake
my senses. It was like
a summons to a man
on his over-stuffed couch:
"Your reading this
indicates your compliance."

I used to clamber to the top
of a hill with my notebook
and watch what the clouds
do over the Pacific coast.
Sometimes I would take
a tape, say, *Sketches of Spain*
or some string quartet
to heighten the effect.

And here would come
a breeze bearing the scent
of Italy or Jamaica—
someplace. The thought
took me away and braced
me to walk home by
snakeskins that bannered
the dry skittering grasses.

It was just escapism,
like browsing the plates
in an art book: Poussin's
"Inspiration," for example,

where "a recumbent poet
unifies everything in soft glazes."
Before the snakes summon
him to the mountain.

But why not escape?
I keep returning for fresh
infusions, remembering,
in every renewable summer
how paradise was air; surely
the music of it was air too,
blossoming from coils
of chlorophyll and brass.

But Spinoza told me
life would be like this,
the best days assembled
in the mind, intellectual
integuments gathering
nerve, for the glaze that
paints the best days black.
That won't come back.

Waiting for the Jews

(after Cavafy)

What are we waiting for, here in the market?

       The Jews will be here any moment.

Why are the banks closed?
Why are the clerks sitting behind glass?

       Because they're waiting for the Jews.
       What's the point of opening for business?
       When the Jews get here, they'll make the deals.

Why did our Leader appear so unexpectedly
on television, sitting behind the Great Seal,
in front of the Flag of State?

       Because the Jews are coming today,
       and the Leader wants to greet their rabbi.
       He's even got Certificates of Citizenship,
       already framed, to give him.

Why have the Mayor and Town Manager come out today
wearing their dark suits and flag lapel buttons?
Why have they put on their diamond-encrusted watches
and rings with the insignia of office?
Why are they carrying the ceremonial gavels,
their bodyguards nervously surveying the crowds?

       Because the Jews are coming today,
       and Jews, we have heard, are keen on glitter.

Why haven't our commentators and pundits
shown up to pontificate and vociferate?

> Because the Jews are coming today,
> and they excel at quarreling and raising their voices.

Why this confused milling about?
(How sad and quiet everyone seems.)
Why is the market being deserted, stalls emptied,
the shop-windows left to mannequins?

> Because it's night and the Jews haven't come.
> And some agents returning from the station say
> there are no Jews any longer. Not anywhere.

What are we going to do now without Jews?
Those people were a kind of solution.

Spaghetti

I had not remembered, but do now.
I'm near the place: the tracks remind me
and the Amtrak horn that precedes
the escaping windows filled with no silhouettes.
It was my last Carolina summer
(money would lure me north)
that I heard the story. It concerned
a mill town early in the century
where a European circus, apropos
of nothing, like all circuses, had turned up.
Imagine how it ignited the margins of town,
not to mention the jaws of the Presbyterians,
whose profiles filled the upper windows.
Farmers looked up from their traces
and saw something extraordinary—
Hannibal's army stopping in the plains.
In this circus was an Italian violinist
who doubled as a hand: two hands
and a spine to hoist the tent, where
circus animals, too ancient for desertion,
doddered to their platforms and roared gamely,
where a ballerina danced on the back
of a treadmill palomino. One night
someone, never caught, shoved a tent-stake
through the violinist's heart. Legend
says a fight over a girl, but who's to know?
The circus vanished like foxfire, leaving
only droppings, the corpse, and some rope.
The coroner confirmed the murder,
and a judge scrawled out a writ.
But here the story gets really interesting.

Shipped to the mortuary, the corpse
was duly embalmed, but unclaimed.
The director, protesting that he
was not in the *pro bono* business,
flatly refused the burial expense.
So the corpse was suffered to wait,
in the manner of corpses, for an act
of charity he was in no position to claim,
though he could be said, posthumously,
to have desired it. Instead, he was removed
in stages to remoter rooms and finally
the attic, where, dried and tanned
as an old billfold, having lost seemingly
his dead weight, he was wired and hung
in a window. Here, he resumed performing,
but this time as a storefront crucifix, taking
upon himself the social lapses of the town.
Framed, the eye-slits and dry mouth
grimaced at the Southern depot platform.
As cracks widen inevitably to chaos, he
acquired a nickname: "Spaghetti." Railway men
and townspeople lined up to have
their pictures taken in the thief positions
by the brown monkey whose loincloth,
flanked by overalls, only hinted at the real
crux of his death, for it bears repeating
that this was the South, where,
from the symbiotic entanglements of debt
and debtor, remembrances and dis-
memberments, you must draw your own
conclusions. Everyone breathed
a complicit air, but at their own expense:

the unburied taking in the laundry
of the never-known, for instance,
if not vice versa. For air,
the great commodity, was all there
would ever be to a story like this.
But the airs of Verdi and Puccini: never
room for them, even after Europe had
given up the importance of self.
The cadaver hung in its window
for *sixty years*, like luck, maybe, or a warning
that we are what we are to others, not
ourselves, hard as the thought is to swallow.
Easier to murder and be damned.

Hosanna

When I turned the corner,
there was something in the road,
its edge flapping like a bag.
A patrol car went by, and I
looked furtively in the rearview,
thinking of the broken headlight
I'd neglected to replace.
But there was enough light.
The possum's spine was broken,
the two halves of its body
working against each other,
clambering for either curb,
getting nowhere. I could hardly
believe my eyes: the gray
pie-slice of its head poised
on the asphalt, its paws rowing
air as if to warn travelers
of an accident, some other
scene of carnage up ahead.
As I drove by, I looked
into the imageless coins of its eyes,
and knew I would turn the corner,
in spite of thickening traffic,
in order to make an end of it.
On my first pass, a thump,
log-like, but I went around again.
I needed to make sure, and there
it was, one paw still waving.
I couldn't get my bearings:
the car missed. And missed
on the next pass, too, as I tried

to line him up where the dead
headlight was. I sickened
at my stupidity and the traffic
suddenly clotting each intersection
as I made the square back.
I knew I must aim for the head,
still facing the oncoming lane.
I switched to high beams, and
the light shot out. He was attempting
to go fetal, but the recalcitrant
spine prevented the lower half
of his body from accomplishing
this. In my vanity of wishes
I spoke to him, asking his
permission just as the left tires
made a double thump, and I knew
there was no point looking back.
Only in the aftermath of failure
can I tell you with what crooked
care I would take my own obliquities
into my hands and smooth them
like a snake straightened into
a cane, the cane compensating
for the grade of the mountain.
Only now can I imagine a word
like *hosanna*, when self-
consciousness escorts
my hulk like a slick,
when sleep is far and bound
for woods—the sticks criss-crossed
in smoky light—for the secret
paths through the underbrush.

A Dawn

As in "Nestus Gurley," the slap
of paper on wall announces
the *Globe*'s wobbly spiral,
the throw's replay connecting
with the jerky, departing silhouette
of the star-child riding his bike
farther into the suburban grid.

The man turns, one foot connects
with the rug, then the torso
asserts its general perpendicular.
As out-of-it as a Depression thug,
he stands before the mirror's
arraignment, which accepts
his image's *nolo contendere*

and offers, from behind its
neutral façade, the special razor
reserved for lifers, monitoring
the condemned's ablutions
as mournfully as a video.
Then the uniform, containing
him, as he emerges and treads

across the grass to the car.
Such drollery in the stars'
departure, such confidence
in the solar right ascension!
The drill of his mother's bones
patterns his steps into a tolerable
destiny, filling his indistinct

envelope with the little gifts
of a rote life, and his father emerges
at the end of a common day
in eternity, and sets down the brown
lunch-bag, triumphantly empty.
But first he must fold the *Globe*
under his arm—good son that he is

up to and including the retinal
surface, where the world impinges
and locks its funhouse image
in the bright reflection of his look,
then carry the frog-pond multiplicity
of worlds into his own, effortlessly,
not letting go, nor letting on.

The End of Romanticism

Something funny was going on inside his head.
He was listening to *Harold in Italy*, the part
where the brass announces the departure
of egotism. Just then, something came down
over his left ear—a kind of net, or blanket
muffling the music and the thoughts
stirred up in him. He turned to the window:
wind searching the leaves. Smoky clouds
scudded in slow, gray twists. He watched cars
splash their way through the streets,
the glassed profiles comical and mysterious.
Would each have known the feeling
of division that suddenly encased him?
Surely it was possible to leap to sympathy
for these strangers, each headed importantly
to a destination: food, a meeting, children, home.
Otherwise, their faces would have turned to see,
through leaves, the same smoky twists
moving into the branches.
They might have wondered, like him,
about the wind above, where the nothing
to be asked is somehow, more than ever,
in view of asking. That "thing" in his head,
was it not a matter of capillaries, which is
to say, the action of routes and exchanges
for blood coming off the mountain
of thought? What kind of thought?
Here he was stumped to characterize
what had brought him
to the window and the cars, though
perhaps it was the same kind of thing

that brought Harold to Italy. Turning
back, he found that he was fine again,
just another being grounded in his
quiddity, as it were. This was not
as death came in Homer, the confusion
permitting non-being to slip in
and down the body, until the knees,
unlatched by chaos, toppled the armored
corpse. This was not even death, just
a turning of no moment, implying nothing
beyond itself. As of clouds, only weather.
What the leaves were about to suggest
in the way of a supposed clarity—just a minor
trick of the light, as blown shadows
rose to shuffle the optic pathways where
nothing came, that briefly stayed
and leaving, left him undefended.

Ex Ponto

In the distance, swallows scissor
a skein of ragged treetops. A wasp
with the wingspan of a buzzard
hangs in the air a moment, then
docks at his paper condominium.
His intractable complex seethes, as clouds
begin to outpuff each other, and a storm
breeze turns the new leaves' hands.

From the balcony I watch the way
the mountains slide into each other
like the precisely made mechanism
of an old camera shutter, until,
at the end-point of sight, the vivid blue
upholds its remote victory sign
like a head of state whose motorcade
negotiates the adoring barbarian throngs.

Ovid despairs from the shores of Russia.
Shall I commiserate, his urban Muse
circumscribed by Caesar's exile?
A weaker Caesar enjoins my scattering
to the terrace honeypot of another's
paradise, where only inertia coordinates
time and place, meanwhile holding
both evasions and rebuttals in check.

May: month beginning every *annus mirabilis*
even here, where reverse baseball caps
herd Camaros into the cramped hollows,
and storms of a sheer American wildness
stain the agnostic blue a meaner purple.

Cleverly reprocessed from servitude
to storm and sun, books, too, lie in exile
from the very nature they would lament,

were it not that someone, somewhere
doubtless let a garden go to seed
because of them. Someone, not me.
The task is to disencumber the tangerine
light that the clouds shade down
into separate darknesses, sealed zones
of affect, chronic obliquity, the dead
ash, after the cigarette's demonic eye.

Or more intensely, to disburden the heavy
in the name of the light on which
it squats, waiting, a mnemonic miser
of no interest to anyone beyond
the hazy outline of his own skin,
preaching to the choir of the self,
privately mad, too arch for responsibility,
this creature slated for destruction.

Inside the mind, a better mind moves
into position; its body ripples down
like a sail, like swallows gashing bolts
of light, so easily do they work the medium.
But Ovid's two lives melt into one book.
Not returning, he finally writes of the snow's
purity and even comes to embrace his neighbor,
whose strange ways and stranger tongue make all

the sense there on that other, that foreign shore.

Rip

Long before a father parked a rented car
under vanishing elms and emerged
hulking, unexceptional, to meet a child
sired like an afterthought whose first inkling
was the image of his own predestined exit,
these were heaven mountains and valleys
ruled impartially by amiable dwarves.

Then, you were my family, until a sleep
worthy of Pirandello, more vertiginous
than the voids cracking before Hudson's men
as they stalked the rippling Palisades, stole us.
Wars came and met our somnolence: slaughter
in the fields and public squares, cries forced
to heaven, followed by snow's immaculate

history, deer crossing the frozen divides,
the years' incessant migration scanned by traffic,
headlights flickering in doubt, then flowing west.
Waking at last to each other's presence, brushing
the other's sleep away, we followed mountains
and valleys, until innocence itself praised us,
and like praise, we gave our happiness away.

Heat

Summer. An ochre light came
from the underside of a storm. Leaves
turned up submissively and shivered.
I saw a plane take off, turn into a crack
in the clouds. Then the crack closed over.
I sat, sweated from my damp scalp,
a secret sweat like condensation on the glass
of a judge who's fallen asleep over a stack
of motions. Lightning jabbed
its emphasis in the vicinity of the water
tower. The river like an arm in a sleeve,
pursued its out-of-body opening.

I saw under the green canopy of vines
the exact sag of the comptroller's jaws
signing his memo on budget cuts, the set
of the Inquisitors when they went to meet
the Cathars at Montségur, comfortless,
without shade. The clouds saw to that:
they willed it so, leaving only the seething
of insects stapled to their rafts of tree bark,
the hot bluster of wind from the lungs
of the coming storm. Sweating like a man
about to be corrected, I considered the rust
blistering the top of the iron tubing

that once supported a clothesline,
likewise the lost clothes hanging in waves,
whose semaphores could have spelled
an unconscious but sweeping critique
of the deepening green, the vanishing blue.

And so on, to beasts of the grass, creaking
with armor, yet programmed for oblivion,
or slinking furtively in their xenophobia,
mindlessness being a plus in any jungle.
Then manic thunder, crazier than Scriabin,
then furious rain for minutes, followed by
waltzing miasmal wisps. Growing legs,

the steam firmed up into figures bound
only to decompress into infinity.
From my hothouse, I watched, as the pageant
swiveled and bobbed, tethered to nothing,
faceless, yet something like persons.
Here, memory grew as delicate and faceless
as bugs, who improved upon people
by hoisting the shields of their skeletons
against grass and stars alike. I sat still
in my flesh, and this flesh reminded me
how it would again translate itself,
faithfully, into another original.

The Exploding Man

A man explodes, showering
walls and floor with himself.
He explodes like an action-painting
in black and red. Even in
the horror of it—the slashes
and looping florets—it is not
unbeautiful. He wishes to be,
in dying, a better artist than death,
to surprise the surprising moment
and twist a blessing from its claw.

Consider how it could have been
otherwise: stoic leave-takings,
moribund whispers, loved ones
metamorphosing into mourners,
the prophetic gray matter overhearing,
"It was just as if he'd left the room,"
as they refold the Afghan over
the emaciated knees. Drooping
in his chaise he would have suffered
a fate worse than life.

Instead, the banshee trucks pull up,
boots stampede through the house.
A radio squawks the vitals'
slipping measurements to Central
as needles shove in, the mask
clamped over the nose: body
reduced to math—but body enough,
and soon the numbers grow.
The exploding man is regrouped:

a Medevac plucks his mass away.

For rescue waits at the window,
monitoring flashpoints from
the *Ready* position, Argus-eyed.
And of all the things perspective
can squeeze, there is this add:
the exploding man packed into
the squares of a poem, and the poem
folded secretly into his dream, carefully
as you may imagine, being a dream.
A merely sick man opens his eyes

later, sees the puzzling bedside faces.
Beyond, low hieroglyphic clouds
melt and redraw themselves.
Nowhere are the stricken reds
and blacks. Only avatars of green.
Now he must be penitently well,
now rejoice at the stacked, knotted bags
that contain his havoc for maggots
and flies—bags of death cinched up,
dragged off by their strangled necks.

The Tufted Grosbeak

The indifferent mother is a tale about clouds
forming and puzzling the forms,
and you may live and die
before her heart, slated to be rent, is formed,
or the clouds settle on the way it was.

Lost in the paradigm of their kind,
the birds of our garden make deities
in the conduits of their song. The tufted grosbeak
was welcomed (or not withstood)
when he came as new, bringing the sound
of what was not into the green,

where the past crests as it weighs
against the present, or the future
intrudes, a storm with no more alibi
than a thug in a nursery.
Whichever way it comes about
the present is presence,
loss though it be.

The Duke of Earl

I descended
my snow-muffled hill
and eased into the highway's
slush and salt-guttered trace.
Oblivious, blinkered,
cars jockeyed for position like thoroughbreds.
I moved into position.
Like a homunculus whose leer
is reflected in the dials,
I pressed a digit
against the array, and the amber window awoke
its digital genie, producing
the imageless, ear-cuffing
FM voice, whose intonations—
seamless, weightless—
warmed the interior with its complicit, cockpit
murmur. Then, passing
cross streets, hurling the already old
slop of snow like spray from a water skier,
I headed for the rest home.

Suddenly, the interior was filled with his absolute
refrain: song that entered the charts thirty
years ago, when, already, I was budding,
hyperventilated. *Already*—the word mortared
thought to thought.
Like a drive-by, snow sprayed
across the façades of buildings.
Wipers working, salt-sludge nevertheless
smoked the glass outside and my breath, inside,
as I drove the long road to the home,

the sinuous Gene Chandler
charming the very rocks
to rise from white fields.

I felt death nearby
in the beauty of erased lawns.
Gene Chandler answered with his cape,
his hobble, assisted, offstage,
the dignity of his aristocratic fantasy,
the image of which time
had hardened into the steadfast.

They hobbled where I was going too
to assist the old in such songs as they had,
such meters as slow time had meted.
With canes and special chairs they came.
Outside it was becoming snow again, already
Already one had written of the brightening windows.
and waved it toward me for approval.
Another had *given up* writing,
and in her stainless conveyance,
died between that snow and this.
The typewriter I brought had no recipient,
and suddenly poetry also meant
no recipient, in some important sense
that we knew, despite our "heightened
consciousness with respect to language"—
that social ideal spread among tables and chairs.
Others took that seat like a place of honor.

And then, quite simply: the long hall
of drawn faces leading to everlasting snow,

the parking lot white, the suspect roads,
even the white fields darkening by now,
and Gene Chandler offstage thirty
pathetic years, in such forbearance
as becomes the silent snow
behind the serenity of Orpheus.

Safe Box

Fresh from contemplating his own death,
now that the cancer, like rain on a carpet,
had upgraded its stain,
my father showed me the gun
my brother used to kill himself.
"Who gave him this thing?" I asked.
"I gave it to him," he said.
"Wish I hadn't done that,"
he added, as he moved to the next item
buried in the safe box.
How could it matter if, with
the defeat of language, he gave it that
smile of sweet patronage
before turning the shell of his torso,
like a drawing,
away from the succeeding view?

Linking Light

Nine months after your suicide,
distracted, I look up from a book
to see the picture window
draw an elemental picture.
A child fills a bucket from the blue
baby's pool and empties it again
with unthinking repetition
into the same pool.
Behind him rises the dark green of woods
where sunlight draws up and stops.
I think: even the image of you is eroding
faster than I can put it away.
The child rises, and for a moment
looks in the direction of my house,
the same moment at which
the setting sun takes brief aim
and its final light strikes his head.

Kiefer, the First Day of Spring

Jill's golden hair ascends
the attic staircase to the studio.
I'm looking at Kiefer: wintry furrows
bearing writing and snow. The human
last seen rising through a stovepipe.
Wind eats the smoke. So:
words in furrows, language planted.

Today, I put my father to bed,
keeping him straight
in the traces of the walker.
Nor did I forget what day it was,
if day can have identity
other than this. My daughter
affirms it, and it is, to her

a brilliant discovery: the first
day of spring. In addition, she has
made her first written story: love
and a princess, some complications,
etc., but coming out fine
in the end, in that kingdom
of pinks and willful purples.

They are colors Kiefer would
have used to suggest disgust.
Jill meanwhile brightens
some blackness that stands
as the default background of things:
mass without definition, the ashen
expectation of board.

Death is awake in the furrows
between color and its absence,
between will and compliance,
snow and language. Without action
on our part, we are leaving the snow
to walk in the traces, to trace
a design there in the background.

A few minutes down the hall,
my father stops to pee, and I
avert my presence by the door.
We are standing in a furrow
the first day of spring. His name
and condition are brightening now,
where light lays open the divide.

In Memory of James Broughton

A drift kicks the stick loose,
sometimes turning, sometimes right—
though the way scarcely matters:
that is matter's motion seen
under the auspices of imaginations
you imagined. I don't know
which was the paradise: this
inconstant perception of grace,
this flesh as bawdy as
the sow's ear of a magnolia petal
turned to catch the western sun,
or the silence of the garden
when evening had hushed
the mating birds. But I do know
it was paradise the trees stood over
when a cardinal's luscious flame
was enveloped in the ancient green,
made or found, as if something
wonderful turned on the difference.

Realm of Day

La Capella San Brizio

Some were escaping the grave,
some were standing around engaged
in the chit-chat of the totally nude,
their buttocks all balled muscle, legs
as taut as grasshoppers' springs but
calmed back into their unsurprising
place above ground. Even those
still skeletons for whom the trumpeting
angels were most exacting labor,
smiled beyond the skull's grimace.

Everything else was less surpassing—
the glory of Christ a gaslit jet
torching similar, but derivative halos.
Here and there Signorelli turned up
moments of indifferent cruelty: Romans
night-sticking poor wretches, for instance.
Even his signature self-portrait reveals
not only Fra Angelico, his friend *al fresco*,
but the struggle of a man mugged and choked
at the unconcerned artists' feet.

Then a pack of German tourists
separated us, as their guide moved
to expound the False Messiah. Their faces
managed an unnerving sameness turning to
the Last Judgment, where devils, like secret
police, joined crowds milling about a piazza
to abduct both tradesmen and their wives.
The rapt spectacles and camera lenses

sheeted to a single, tilted pane such as
the sun flares in evening windows.

At which point I drew my hand
to my face and discovered there
the morning's morning sex unwashed
enough to enter a Duomo, like the ardor
of those bodies, for whom spirit and flesh
were never wholly distinguished,
except to instruct the sight-impaired,
for whom dark was history's likeness,
and God's painted head: a flashlight
jabbing the smoke and rubble.

Sonnet

Great banks of windows only brought
suit-gray of winter green closer, canted
trunks and painterly bark, scales of ivy
under nude limbs whose colors qualified
as silhouette whether sky were slate
or no. Every so often thought-like breezes
would pass, stirring out-of-reach greenery
and palmy ferns. Then all was still again,
trees tall and empty—tall *because* empty
in the A-framed window (not all transparency
pointing to heaven). Here, some offered alternate
accounts of how darkness took up with glass,
how dead ones could be buried in our talk,
that silence might leave us otherwise moved.

Dream Oration

Asked to give the funeral oration for my father,
I discover I have no shirt and the ceremony
is in ten minutes. Forget the shirt. I focus
on a narrative thread that will stitch three parts
into a whole for, it seems, the benefit of my students
just now arriving from their farms, filling the athletic
arena with the wary families I observed as a child,
arranged like movie tableaux on their rotting porches.
Mounting the stage, clutching to my chest the few
sheets I haven't time to write, I adjust the microphone
and peer out onto darkened rows, feeling behind me
the doctors fanning themselves in their stifling regalia.
"The crickets," I begin, "played their quartet
in better days and minds. And when death contested
their songs, they regrouped and lived the winter
basking in the glow of a furnace, anonymously tended."
I put down the white pages and leave the hall, snatching
my shirt, fleece-like, from a hook at the entrance
and departing down a towpath, trailed by horseflies,
passing the cemetery where new stones are being
mortared into place. Two workmen wave trowels
and I recognize the taller one as a schoolmate.
In fact, I see that I am headed for the schoolhouse,
site of honor for my father, for whose three tenses
I set the healing metronome and learned to dress
history in figures—as dreams told us they were.
In my dream I trail as close to silence as words
allow, when they first attempt to chalk,
after its departure, the body's outline. I woke,
but no daytime could repair its monochrome.
Sunlight struck sacred and trifling plots

at the same time: my poetry books stacked
like mail trashed on the night table,
obscuring a hodgepodge of photographs.
In my eulogy's wake still roared a double silence
for the body's two bodies: my dead father
in a dream. And my dead father.

Wild Strawberries

Finches in the clothesline post
fall silent as I make my way along
the ground, the coiled vines,
mulch, dead sticks strewn
among darkening ground cover.
A groundhog comes this way
after crawling slowly, unafraid,
over the yard like a mist doing
its abracadabra over a lake.
Honeysuckle, black raspberry,
and wild grape sag from the fence.
Limbs smashed from the hurricane
prop against vines, and, paying
no mind to that past, green
and tender, they reach to begin
coiling up dead bark. I rip and saw,
lift armloads of viney green
to the fence and lay it over.
I wonder how last week's doe
made the thicket melt, her white tail
a flat hand as permanently trite
as a waving beauty queen's. I decapitate
pokeweed, slash that sham bigness,
throw it on top of a wall of trash.
Here and there poison oak
shoulders through: haughty,
overripe—a road company soprano—
expanding under the auspices
of pecan, cherry, and fir, whose
interposed limbs thwart its union
with sunlight. A finch

squawks from the trash pile,
making a big deal of my notice.
I work my way closer to her chicks
packed into their iron tube.
Through a daylily I can see her
wrenching in melodrama,
and I know I crouch in violation
of her express rules, a Caliban
who spreads his shadow through
the state-space of another's ecstasy.
Over my shoulder bees and bugs
dart, mercurial, through cylinders
of light. Others plunge entirely
into faces of flowers or rumble
through loam. A worm
awakened by a hoe blade
stirs like the time-lapse
of a tendril too young to name.
The possum lurks somewhere who
grimaced in the headlights.
Bats sleep in their cupboard,
undisturbed by the family
of squirrels on patrol from their drains,
tending to outrage, and trigger-happy
when the boorish bluejay swells nearby.
Consonant with every quickness,
whether it stays or goes,
they occupy a rotted corner
where, below and cool, skunks
sleep, who fear for nothing—
a queen and her sable kittens.
More limbs to come down,

more sticks and briars
to pluck and drag, strangling
weeds to find and root up
so that the wild strawberries
get a chance to offer up their
plump rubies before they perish
from contact with the earth,
like apples and peaches,
whole sides that lay there,
spoiling where you can't see,
complicit with their slow decay.
These are wasted utterly to air,
which is all fruition, blazing
where the light races, mashing
the world along its stupefying edge,
earth's edge, along which I creep.

Stefano

(dead in Rome, 2002)

Chianti and vodka. Porcini tossed
in steaming cords of pasta.
Everyone who came through the door was met
with your dash to the cucina,
wit countered with food,
class met by its isotope, style.
Hospitality proved everyone at length
an exile. It was your talent,
after years and worlds to equate
the walk-in with the friend,
the stranger with the family
you would not have. But houses
and habitués were your line:
to each an assignable place.
Your job and life merged more neatly
than the bratty painters and poets
gobbling the spreads at your famous parties
before swarming the corners where
some spidery countess or other still held court.
In that world of casual, contrived
rendezvous you found sweet order
a Wilde would have admired,
dancing mask-to-mask, who
were otherwise a long-ago injured child
nauseated by the turning of the knob,
parents' return, the grinding of keys.

Umbrian Odes

in memory of Joseph Brodsky

I.

Stacked stone holds its cutout against the blue.
Old window arches are bricked, having
been first covered with concrete
and that slagged off. Swallows loop
from cracks to air and back, and pigeons
perched like gargoyles gentle into sleepy,
perishable sentries. What is looked at persists
as the seen, in archaic recirculation.

Was this the old structure of the world—
to rise skyward on the sturdy back of matter?
Or was the ambition less, the organized
rubble only keeping pace with bodies?
As it happens, we are sitting by a pool
discussing cloth's impersonations of flesh.
While I like the indolence of silk, you
like the thing itself, even when it is

the shirt stuffed, a movement container.
The bald, smoking father orders
his cowed girls around the water. Enough
of the centurion survives his linteled brow
and granite nose to explain more
than towers, but he seems out of place,
subdued by his offspring's gaucherie,
as if the facial bearing were indifference's

rebuttal. A boatload of Darwins

could not console him for the arrival
of the rich couple and their aquiline,
disheveled children whose nearly
rotted innocence alerts the pornographer's
instrument. He knows they are closer
to stone than he and quick to assume
the *castelli* for their backdrop needs.

You hint that silk is a good thing because
it forces one to admit that violence
begets taste, if only that to pose words
in the manner of our sentience is to have
left capriciously on a long journey.
Like lying on our deathbeds, I add.
At which point, the pool takes, like
Narcissus, heaven's emptiness for itself.

II.

In sunlight, the landscape reverses Corot:
the front field of vision bright,
a hillside of attentive sunflowers, followed
by some darker stand of green—what life
summer puts in the way of life: ennui
of leaf-weight! An unstruggling tangle of grass
promises the skink to go with the hare.
Summer cancels and dispenses indifferently,
as the artist knew, who framed golden clearings
from the nearer embrace of indistinct

branches sedged with bitten leaves
and spotted fruit, Romantic props for a time
when selves let nature interrogate their
obscurity, wondering when the ball of gnats
would land or whether two sizes of viper
supported the theory that lower phyla
traveled *en famille*. Impossible, then, to turn
the sunflowers away from an allegory
of sunflowers, to resist thinking that
such doughty sunlight belonged to the past

and that things tightened up a bit once
the creek marked the sloping field's edge.
Perhaps old fields were always in the business
of leading the eye to the edge of the page,
after a sleep of fantastic flowers—
that felt you were watching them
through the page's tiny bars, and the change
that came over your face was like
a cloud that drifted behind your blown hair
and set by the roof of the old toolshed.

III.

Plow and harvest over the dead
and summer sunlight falling straight.
This, and the yolk competes with the fields
of sunflowers standing precisely at salute
until their fingers curl, but not the yellow.
The hog's destiny resembles the poem's,
in its way superior to the empty churches
watched over by the local police.

Fruits swell faster than a cloud.
Better to let them spot and fall, food
for wasps and inchworms making an alphabet
through alimentary canals. Like paratroopers
peas strap-hang the whole length of July,
and when wheat exits via the dirt road
beside the beheaded grass, an owl is in
no better position than the useless twig

a canopy covered for. Gnawed by beetles,
sooted by harvest's systematic monsters,
a broadleaf sallies forth into Diesel air:
everywhere the same leaf claims its solar
privilege upon mountainous racks of the dead,
so sturdily inanimate that no question
can ever break through to the obtuse skulls
of the unfallen animals. But a farmer

sits in his cab as the truck pulls round
with its gaping hopper. Trailed by swallows
and a floating wake of dust, he pauses
to wipe the rearview mirror, his hand
extending to the window of the beast,
returning to cradle his own jaw that houses
his toothache, while his colleagues look on
and finish the lunch, that turns into siesta.

IV.

Trees and hedgerows, like an ink trail,
rewrite the hills into that realistic novel,
Joseph, you thought the last century had missed.

Of the three segments of a vodka bottle, the first,
alone, seems incapable of bestowing poetry. Three
balls of gnats juggle for the favor of an apricot tree.
The local group, a few feet before my face,
give both force and nuance to the evening breeze.
Doves start up behind me, intoning
the bare syllable of their stony comfort.

A blue bus negotiates the road to town,
in which the cappuccino keeps dendrites
from drooping into winter kudzu.
Neither is the white car put off by geology.
The spiral up holds no improvement, save
the way down, etc. Consistency beats out surprise
in land, as in cuisine, eliminating any shadow
that would streak the yolk. Say what you will,
the mind pulls back from the brink in time
to switch either Tyson or Titian for *Lucy*.

Every day the Duomo tower indicates nothing
but diversifying clouds pulling back to reveal
a sky depopulated of everything save more clouds
and the occasional raptor touring emptiness
like Satan savoring the chaos. The wasp felt
a reassurance, that bare thermal pillar,
though once the grub's aspirations ranged across
the sexy fuzz of a peach. Epic vacillations
require hexameters designed to scythe
any shape that comes down the pike.

As for us, our best lines lie in canceled stanzas,
no doubt, homogenized by a silence as thick

as ennui. Let the thought, like a grub, climb out
the tops of our peach fuzz, for otherwise,
how keep past vividness from sinking to a level
that lets mediocrities step forward as maestros?
Existence merely arrived, Parnassian, but not
Parnassus. Still, a few molecules peeled from
the aqueduct, and pretty soon the whole Empire
faded before the more ancient snow of a television.

V.

When I turn, you are gone,
and it doesn't matter if I specify
the number of chairs, or simply
imply a renewed brightness around
the edge of the pool. No one observes
the mirror held to heaven. The sun
is having to work today, gesso
clouds refigure portions of sky.

Soon the whole. Meanwhile, I have
identified the dry sound, something
between a chitter and a buzz, by which
grasses hold forth when light eases.
A grasshopper, like a sprinter in his blocks,
kicks one hind leg into motion,
is answered by another enthusiast
not bound by sight, elsewhere in the yard.

In the distance, elemental thunder
expounds its critique against the eye's
regime, the regime of Piero and Cimabue,

who understood that the spectacle
of the hanged man secured meaning,
which is to say, proportion and difference,
crossing the retinal threshold to take
up residence in the soft place of matter.
Now, amphibian belchings intersect
but don't combine with birds' litanies.
My daily interventions inchworm across
the paper's flatland on their way to you:
but how oblique still, to the daisy's silent,
unmediated thrust that takes it a little bit
toward the sun, after having shouldered
its stuff above the paving stones.

David Rigsbee was educated at the University of North Carolina at Chapel Hill, the Johns Hopkins University, Hollins College, and the University of Virginia. The most recent of his nine previous books is *Invited Guest: An Anthology of Twentieth-Century Southern Poetry* (co-edited with Steven Ford Brown). His awards include fellowships and prizes from the National Endowment for the Arts, Virginia Commission on the Arts, the Fine Arts Work Center at Provincetown, and the Academy of American Poets. His work has appeared in such places as *The New Yorker, Poetry,* and *American Poetry Review.*